# THE BIRTH OF THE
# MOTOR CAR

USBORNE PUBLISHING

## Acknowledgements

We wish to thank the following individuals and organizations for their assistance and for making available material in their collections.

Key to picture positions:
(T) top, (C) centre, (B) bottom,
(L) left, (R) right.

American History Picture Library, 40(L), 41(CL, CR)
Autocar, 19(TL)
Deutsches Museum, 6(BR)
Dunlop Ltd, 13(TL)
Esso Petroleum Company Ltd, 39(BR)
Ford Motor Company Ltd, 39(TR)
Illustrated London News, 31(TC, TR, CL, C)
Mary Evans Picture Library, 7(BL, BR), 15(TL, TR), 16(L), 17(BR)
Michelin Tyre Company Ltd, 13(TR)
National Motor Museum, Beaulieu, 17(TR), 19(TR, CR), 39(TL, C, BL)
Posthumus, Cyril, 38(TR, BR)
Radio Times Hulton Picture Library, 13(CL), 17(CL, CR, BL), 29(B second from left), 31(TL, CR), 38(CL)
Renault Ltd, 17(TL), 38(BC)
Roberts, Peter, 11(C), 13(R), 34(T), 38(BL)
Shell International Petroleum Company Ltd, 38(CR)

We would also like to thank the following for their help in the preparation of this book:
British Leyland (Austin-Morris) Ltd
Chrysler UK Ltd
Keith Fletcher

## Illustrators

Roland Berry
Bernard Blatch
Sydney Cornford
   (Gilchrist Studios)
Bob Cosford
Bill Easter
Roger Full
Keith Robson
Lawrence Taylor
George Thompson
Michael Woods

## Editor

Jenny Tyler

## Designers

Bob Scott
Peter Wakeford

## Picture Manager

Millicent Trowbridge

## Picture Researcher

Tessa Campbell

## Typesetting

Garland Graphics, Bristol

## Colour Reproduction

Fotolitho Drommel, Zandvoort, Holland

**Made and printed in England** by
W. S. Cowell Ltd, Butter Market, Ipswich

First published in 1976 by
Usborne Publishing Ltd
20 Garrick Street
London WC2

© 1976 Usborne Publishing Ltd

ISBN 0 86020 024 8

# THE BIRTH OF THE
# MOTOR CAR

PHILIP SUMNER & JENNY TYLER

One of the first cars produced by the Rolls-Royce partnership. It was made in 1905.

# CONTENTS

# Before the Motor Car

A hundred years ago it was not uncommon for people to die without ever having travelled more than ten miles or so from their homes. Horse-drawn transport was slow and very uncomfortable, particularly in country areas where the roads were just muddy, rutted tracks. The best roads were paved with cobbles, but they were still bumpy and uneven. In towns traffic and pedestrians mingled all over the roads.

There were privately owned carriages large and small, commercial vehicles designed to carry goods of all descriptions, and public transport vehicles for those who could not afford their own carriages.

4

**1** Only rich people could afford to keep large carriages. This type was called a barouche. It was always driven by a coachman, never by the owner, and usually kept for important occasions.

**2** Two-wheeled private vehicles of this type were called buggies or gigs. They carried one or two passengers and were often pulled by a pony.

**3** For long-distance travel there were stage coaches. Average speeds were only 8 to 10 m.p.h., so long journeys could take days. The seats were hard and people were squashed close together.

**4** Hansom cabs were used as taxis. Fares were about twice as much as bus fares.

**5** The demand for public transport grew as towns increased in size. Double-decker horse-drawn omnibuses first appeared in the 1850s and proved very successful.

**6** Drays were a type of vehicle used for carrying beer barrels. They were sometimes pulled by four horses as shown here and sometimes by two large horses which were harnessed one behind the other and urged along by drovers walking alongside.

**7** The fastest method of transport was riding on horseback.

**8** Handcarts were widely used in towns for carrying luggage short distances.

**9** A popular type of private coach was the landau which was named after the German town where it was first made. Landaus usually seated four people, and had hoods front and back which could be folded down in fine weather.

5

# Wind and Steam Vehicles

A great many inventors applied themselves to the problem of how to make a vehicle go without the use of animals. Several of them thought of using the wind. But the wind is too unreliable and variable to be of very much use.

Towards the end of the 17th century, people began to realize that steam could be used to make things go. Engines which worked by steam forcing a piston up and down in a cylinder were used by a number of experimenters to turn the wheels of a vehicle. Some of the more successful experiments are shown on these pages.

**1600** Sailing carriages were used in China thousands of years ago. But the first ones seen in the Western world were made in Holland around 1600. This one was built by a Dutchman called Simon Stevin and was able to carry 28 passengers. It worked very well when the wind blew in the right direction.

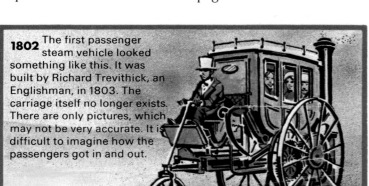

**1802** The first passenger steam vehicle looked something like this. It was built by Richard Trevithick, an Englishman, in 1803. The carriage itself no longer exists. There are only pictures, which may not be very accurate. It is difficult to imagine how the passengers got in and out.

**1804** Oliver Evans, an American, was experimenting with steam at the same time as Trevithick. In 1804, he built a steam vehicle which could go on land and in water. It was for dredging harbours.

**1827** Carriages pulled by one or more kites were made in the 1820s by Viney and Pocock of England. They also planned to build a platform on the back of these carriages to carry a small horse in case the wind failed.

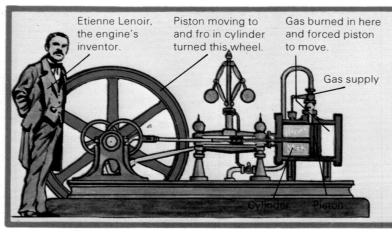

**1833** This small steam coach was built by Maceroni and Squire. It ran a passenger service in London for a while.

Etienne Lenoir, the engine's inventor.

Piston moving to and fro in cylinder turned this wheel.

Gas burned in here and forced piston to move.

Gas supply

Cylinder    Piston

**1859** Early in the 19th century several people realized that if a gas was set alight in a closed cylinder it could force a piston to move. Among the substances tried as fuel were hydrogen gas, turpentine and gunpowder.

In 1859, Lenoir built an engine that used gas from the mains supply lit by an electric spark. It was called an internal combustion engine because the fuel was burnt *inside* it.

**1860** Nicholas Otto, a German scientist, perfected what is known as the four-stroke internal combustion engine. This type of engine is used in most cars today.

**1649** This vehicle was made in Germany. Its "engine" was a number of men hidden inside turning handles.

**1769** A French engineer called Nicholas Cugnot seems to have built the first full-sized steam vehicle. It was designed to tow guns for the army. The heavy boiler at the front made it hard to steer and it is supposed to have crashed. Cugnot built a second vehicle in 1771, but it was so slow the army lost interest.

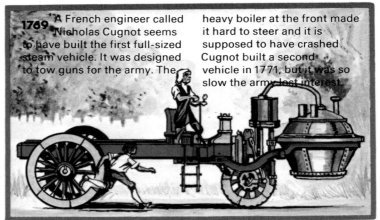

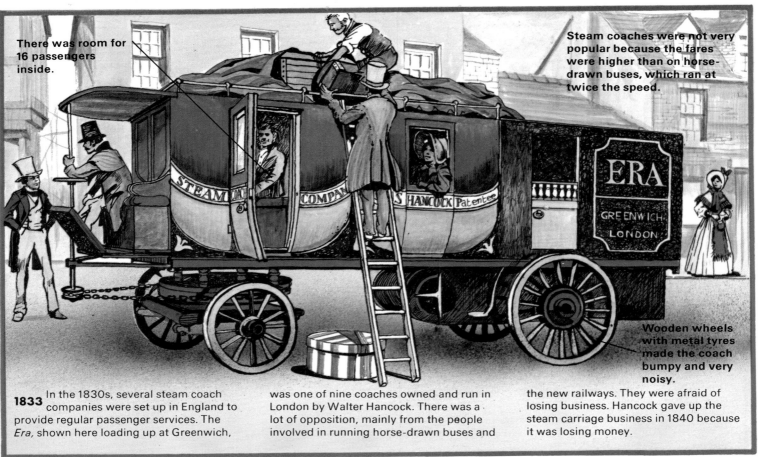

There was room for 16 passengers inside.

Steam coaches were not very popular because the fares were higher than on horse-drawn buses, which ran at twice the speed.

ERA

GREENWICH LONDON

Wooden wheels with metal tyres made the coach bumpy and very noisy.

**1833** In the 1830s, several steam coach companies were set up in England to provide regular passenger services. The *Era*, shown here loading up at Greenwich, was one of nine coaches owned and run in London by Walter Hancock. There was a lot of opposition, mainly from the people involved in running horse-drawn buses and the new railways. They were afraid of losing business. Hancock gave up the steam carriage business in 1840 because it was losing money.

**1861** A few private steam vehicles appeared in the late 1850s. This one was built by Thomas Rickett, an Englishman. A stoker (in French, *chauffeur*) had to be employed to keep the boiler going.

**1878** Amedée Bollée, a Frenchman, began building steam carriages in the late 1870s. This one was built in 1878.

# The First Oil Wells

The ancient Egyptians are known to have used oil that seeped out of the ground for greasing their chariot wheels and mummifying dead bodies. The Romans used this oil too, and called it "petroleum", from their words *petra*, meaning rock, and *oleum*, meaning oil.

Petroleum is thought to have formed from the dead bodies of tiny salt-water plants and animals that were squashed and buried under layers of rock and earth. Movements in the layers brought some of the oil to the surface, where it formed little pools.

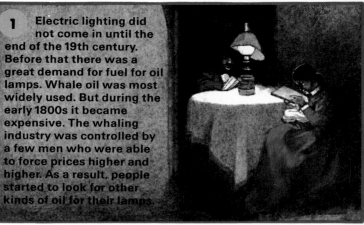

**1** Electric lighting did not come in until the end of the 19th century. Before that there was a great demand for fuel for oil lamps. Whale oil was most widely used. But during the early 1800s it became expensive. The whaling industry was controlled by a few men who were able to force prices higher and higher. As a result, people started to look for other kinds of oil for their lamps.

The first oil well

**4** Drillers looking for salt water in America sometimes found oil, but the first man to drill for *oil* was a Colonel Drake in 1858.

**5** The first thing Drake's men found when they started drilling was water, which gushed out all over them.
In August the following year they were drilling in a place called Titusville in Pennsylvania. Suddenly they struck a large quantity of oil. Immediately, they began pumping it up and collecting it in old tin cans and anything else that was lying around.

**8** The method used for drilling was very primitive. A heavy piece of metal was hung from one end of a springy pole. Two men jerked the pole up and down, driving the metal into the ground.

The other end of the pole was attached to the ground some distance away.

This man turned the drill round now and again so that it made a round hole.

Each man put his foot through a rope loop attached to the pole.

**9** A slightly different method of drilling involved the operator jumping up and down on a spring-board which was tied to the springy pole. This picture shows a cross-section of a well being drilled.
A   Spring-pole, usually a sapling 40-50 feet long.
B   Rope attaching spring-pole to jump-board.
C   Operator jumping up and down made the drill move up and down.
D   Man who made sure the drill moved straight.
E   Rope attached to drill.
F   Pit dug down as far as solid rock and lined to prevent it from caving in.
G   Heavy metal drill. Constant banging forced drill through the rock.

**2** Whale oil comes from a layer of fat, called blubber, which surrounds whales' bodies. 19th century whalers killed the whale with harpoons, then towed it to a ship for the blubber to be stripped off.

**3** Some American Indians found petroleum and used it for medicine and fuel. They collected it by soaking blankets in the oil pools and wringing them out over their storage pots.

**6** William A. (Uncle Billy) Smith actually did the drilling of Drake's well. He was an experienced driller of deep salt-water wells.

**7** The news of Drake's success spread rapidly. People began drilling all over the place and many of them found oil.

**10** Oil from the early wells was pumped into large open vats. It was then run off into wooden barrels, each holding about 35 gallons. The output of an oil well is still measured in barrels per day.

**11** The filled barrels were often floated down river to waiting ships. Some ships' crews refused to sail when they found that the cargo was oil because they were frightened of it catching fire.

**12** An early oil refinery. Petrol was a waste product and was burnt. The heavier oil was kept.

**13** John D. Rockefeller was one of the people who made a fortune out of oil. Drake died a poor man.

# The First Cars

By the 1860s, there were engines small enough and light enough to fit into a vehicle and fuel for them that was portable and cheap. All that was needed was someone to see their potential and put them together in a car. It is hard to say who was the first person to build a car, but it seems almost certain that the first person to do so *and* to realize the importance of what he had done was Karl Benz, a German engineer.

Benz had been building gas engines for several years, but he knew that they were too unwieldy to be useful in vehicles, and so concentrated his efforts on petrol engines. By 1884 he was ready to put one of his engines into a vehicle. He designed and built a light three-wheeler specially for the purpose, and by the following year his car was completed. From that time on, anyone who had enough money could buy a car.

Gottlieb Daimler, another German engineer, was also experimenting with petrol-engined vehicles at this time. Communications were so bad that though Benz and Daimler lived only about 60 miles apart, neither knew about the other's work. Daimler had developed his own internal combustion engine and in 1885 fitted it to a bicycle. The next year he bought an ordinary carriage (meant to be pulled by a horse), removed the shafts and put in an engine. This was Daimler's first experiment with a car. Three years later he too was building cars for sale.

▶ **Benz took his first car** out onto the road towards the end of 1885.

By 1888, when the Benz cars were advertised for sale, there was still no-one interested enough to want to buy one. Later that year, however, Frau Benz and her two sons made a 70-mile journey by themselves while Karl was away. Their trip turned out to be good publicity for Benz. Orders began to come in because men decided that if a woman and two children could manage a car it must be very easy.

**To start the engine, the heavy flywheel had to be jerked round in a clockwise direction.**

**This started the piston moving to and fro in the cylinder. Petrol vapour was sucked in as the piston moved in.**

**A spark exploded the compressed petrol and the force of the explosion started the piston moving by itself.**

**Starting could take fifteen minutes or more in cold weather.**

To the left of the driver was a lever for moving leather belt from loose drum to fixed drum (and thus starting the car moving).

The engine had one cylinder only. (Most modern cars have 4 or 6). It was mounted sideways instead of upright.

Petrol tank.

Benz knew that the engine would need a lot of attention, so he placed it where it could be reached easily from all sides.

Heavy metal flywheel, attached to the engine.

Leather belt.

Wire-spoked wheels, like bicycle wheels.

One half of this drum was fixed to a rod which turned when the engine was going. The other half was loose. When the belt was on the loose part of the drum, the car wheels were not driven.

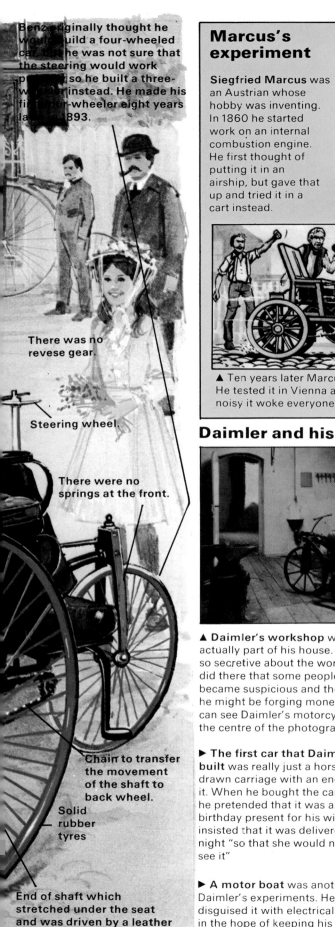

Benz originally thought he would build a four-wheeled car, but he was not sure that the steering would work properly, so he built a three-wheeler instead. He made his first four-wheeler eight years later, in 1893.

There was no revese gear.

Steering wheel.

There were no springs at the front.

Chain to transfer the movement of the shaft to back wheel.

Solid rubber tyres

End of shaft which stretched under the seat and was driven by a leather belt from the engine.

## Marcus's experiment

Siegfried Marcus was an Austrian whose hobby was inventing. In 1860 he started work on an internal combustion engine. He first thought of putting it in an airship, but gave that up and tried it in a cart instead.

▲ One night he pushed the cart to a lonely lane, started the engine and jumped in.

▲ After a few yards the cart broke down. So he pushed it home again and forgot about it for a while.

▲ Ten years later Marcus built another car. He tested it in Vienna at night, but it was so noisy it woke everyone up.

▲ Eventually the police ordered Marcus to stop his motoring activities. He obeyed and turned his mind to other inventions. It was left to Benz to develop a workable motor car.

## Daimler and his engine

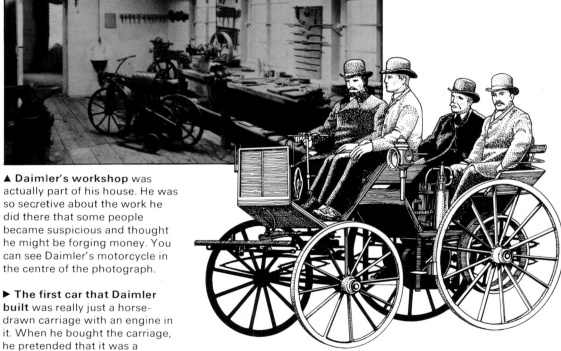

▲ Daimler's workshop was actually part of his house. He was so secretive about the work he did there that some people became suspicious and thought he might be forging money. You can see Daimler's motorcycle in the centre of the photograph.

▶ The first car that Daimler built was really just a horse-drawn carriage with an engine in it. When he bought the carriage, he pretended that it was a birthday present for his wife and insisted that it was delivered at night "so that she would not see it"

▶ A motor boat was another of Daimler's experiments. He disguised it with electrical wires in the hope of keeping his idea a secret.

# Motoring Moves to France

The Paris World Fair of 1888 contained two German exhibits that hardly anyone took note of apart from two French machinery manufacturers called René Panhard and Emile Levassor. The exhibits were the latest Daimler and Benz cars. In the next three years Panhard and Levassor acquired the rights to make Daimler engines in France and built cars of two different designs.

In the meantime, Armand Peugot, a friend of Levassor's had also become interested in the Daimler engines. Peugot's family had a big ironmongery business. It was quite easy for them to adapt to making car bodies in which they could put engines bought from Panhard and Levassor. The cars they made were in fact some of the first French cars available for sale.

Armand Peugot proved to be a marvellous salesman. In 1891 he entered one of his cars in a race – the Paris to Brest cycle race. It was not even close to beating the cyclists, but it did complete the journey. Sales increased enormously.

So many people set themselves up as motor car manufacturers in France over the next few years that, by the end of the century, France had taken over from Germany as the main motoring nation. The first races for cars were organized by the French, held in France and won by French cars.

## The story of the pneumatic tyre

Pneumatic tyres were first used on a car in 1895 by the Michelin brothers of France. The tyres kept puncturing, but the car went very well when they did hold air. By 1904, pneumatics had taken over from solid rubber tyres. Dunlop made the first pneumatic cycle tyres in 1888, but he was not the first to think of them. Thomson had made an inflatable rubber tyre 40 years before but it had been forgotten.

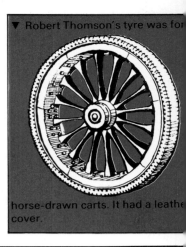

▼ Robert Thomson's tyre was for horse-drawn carts. It had a leather cover.

## The first "modern" car layout

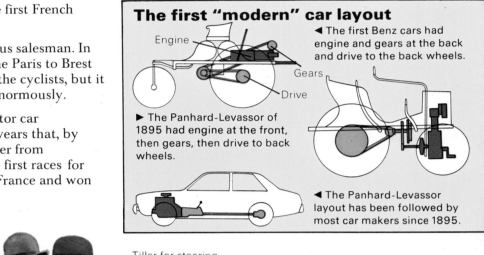

Engine

◄ The first Benz cars had engine and gears at the back and drive to the back wheels.

Gears

Drive

► The Panhard-Levassor of 1895 had engine at the front, then gears, then drive to back wheels.

◄ The Panhard-Levassor layout has been followed by most car makers since 1895.

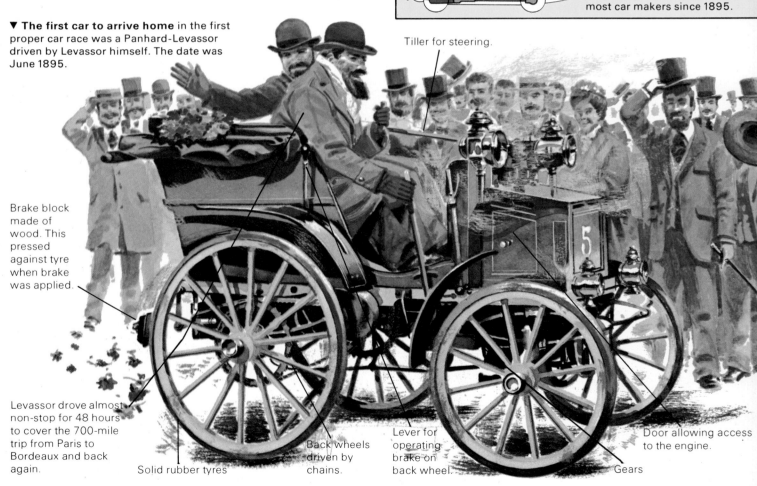

▼ **The first car to arrive home** in the first proper car race was a Panhard-Levassor driven by Levassor himself. The date was June 1895.

Tiller for steering.

Brake block made of wood. This pressed against tyre when brake was applied.

Levassor drove almost non-stop for 48 hours to cover the 700-mile trip from Paris to Bordeaux and back again.

Solid rubber tyres

Back wheels driven by chains.

Lever for operating brake on back wheel.

Door allowing access to the engine.

Gears

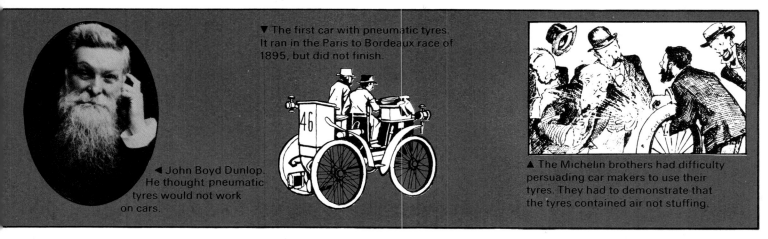

▼ The first car with pneumatic tyres. It ran in the Paris to Bordeaux race of 1895, but did not finish.

◀ John Boyd Dunlop. He thought pneumatic tyres would not work on cars.

▲ The Michelin brothers had difficulty persuading car makers to use their tyres. They had to demonstrate that the tyres contained air not stuffing.

▲ Charles Rolls, who was famous for the cars he built with Royce, photographed in his first racing car. It was the Panhard-Levassor of 1898, fitted with pneumatic tyres. (Notice the spare tyres tied onto the side of the car.)

The driver's partner, René Panhard.

Madame Levassor, Emile's wife.

WILHIO.

▲ A poster advertising the cars of the French firm De Dion -Bouton. This type of car was called *vis-a-vis,* which means face to face, because of the way the passengers sat. The driver had to look over the heads of the people opposite him. The poster was produced in the 1890s.

# American and British Pioneers

The cars made by Benz and Daimler did not excite much enthusiasm in their own country at first. They made even less impact on people in America and Britain. Nevertheless, by the early 1890s both these countries were beginning to develop their own motor cars.

Progress was slow in America because roads outside the towns were so bad – they consisted mainly of mud and rock – and distances between the towns were so enormous. Cars had to be particularly strong and reliable to cope with these conditions.

The first American cars for sale were made by Charles and Frank Duryea. Their cars looked like horse-drawn buggies without horses, which is more or less what they were. The Duryea brothers made their own engines, but from 1891 Daimler engines were being made and sold in Long Island, New York. The makers, named Steinway, were actually more famous for their pianos.

In Britain there was a great deal of opposition to any kind of road vehicle not pulled by a horse. Motor vehicles were not allowed to go faster than four miles an hour, which is about walking pace. Even then there had to be someone walking in front with a red flag to warn people. Those who might have experimented with motor cars were discouraged.

**▼ The Oldsmobile Curved Dash** was typical of the early American cars. It was simple, but rugged, and had bodywork and engine high off the ground to avoid damage from rough roads.

Olds was one of the first people to make cars in large numbers. He made the first Curved Dashes in 1901 and sold 500 of them that year. This was one of about 5,000 that he made in 1903.

Starting handle, which had to be given a sharp turn in a clockwise direction.

Petrol tank was inside this box. It held about five gallons.

**▶ One of the problems with steam cars** was that they used a lot of water – about a gallon a mile. This car had a special device for sucking water from streams, which saved the driver from having to carry heavy buckets.

Engine was started by lighting the petrol burner with a match.

Inside here was a tank for petrol. People often think that steam-powered vehicles need to carry a pile of coal for heating the water. In fact, most successful steam cars used petrol for this.

Car was steered by moving this handle (called a tiller) to the left for turning right and to the right for turning left.

**▲ Three-quarters of the cars sold in America** in 1899 did not have internal combustion engines. They were run by steam or electric engines. This one was a steam car. The passengers were the car's makers, the identical Stanley twins. They always dressed exactly alike and even trimmed their beards the same way.

The Curved Dash got its name from this curly piece of wood at the front. It was called Oldsmobile after its maker Ransom Eli Olds.

A hood was sometimes fixed to the back of the seat.

The engine was under the seat. It had one cylinder.

The distance between the two front wheels was the same as on a horse-drawn cart. This allowed it to use the cart tracks in muddy roads.

▲ **In Paris, electric cars were used as taxis.** This cartoon shows a training course for new taxi drivers. It had every kind of road surface, two steep hills and plenty of cardboard pedestrians to test the drivers.

▶ **Thomas Edison,** inventor of the phonograph and the electric light bulb, displays the batteries in his first electric car. Edison thought that his new type of battery would solve all the problems associated with electric cars and put petrol cars out of business. It did not work as well as he had hoped.

▲ **Electric cars were clean and quiet** but their batteries needed re-charging every few miles. They were useful only in towns where a charging station like this one was not too far away.

Stamp commemorating the 100th anniversary of Henry Ford's birth. The car is Ford's Model A of 1903. Ford was later associated with cheap cars, but this one cost $100 more than a 1903 Cadillac.

Lanchester's father.

Frederick's younger brother George, who later ran the car business. Frederick had too many other interests – like studying Wagner and aviation and painting pottery.

▼ **Frederick Lanchester,** a brilliant young British engineer, built England's first successful four-wheeled car in 1895. Before this he had been designing flying machines, but decided that the time had not yet come for an engine to fly. The car shown here is a Lanchester of 1897.

Hinged apron to protect driver and passengers.

Lanchester thought that when people drove in a car their eyes should be the same height above the ground as they were when they were walking along. He built his cars accordingly.

The Lanchester cars looked old-fashioned even when they were new. People did not want to buy them for this reason, though they were technically very advanced.

# The New Danger

From the ordinary person's point of view, motor cars were noisy, smelly monsters that disturbed their peace and did no good whatever. The police were often of the same opinion. They set speed traps and fined motorists for the slightest infringement of the law.

People were used to the speed of horse-drawn vehicles, which never went faster than about 20 m.p.h. When they saw motor vehicles approaching they did not realize that they could be travelling at perhaps three times this speed. Playing "chicken" became a popular pastime among children. The last one to cross the road before a car went past was the winner. They even did it during races. Animals were dangerous too. They were used to having roads to themselves and were caught unawares by fast motors.

## A race which did not finish

The fact that motor cars could be extremely dangerous was effectively demonstrated by the first big racing disaster. It was in 1903 and the cars were to race from Paris to Madrid – the longest race ever held up to that time. There were no barriers to keep people and animals off the roads. Drivers were blinded by the dust that was thrown up. The result was several dead and many injured among drivers and spectators. The race was eventually abandoned half way through. Following this, legislation was introduced to prohibit motor racing on open roads.

▲ **As cars went faster** and there were more of them, the chance of a serious accident increased. This terrible head-on collision was reported in a French magazine on August 18, 1907. It is not certain whether anyone was killed. Brakes on cars of this time were usually very poor and operated on only two of the four wheels. Sudden emergency stops were just not possible.

## A motorist's nightmare

▼ Cartoonists often made fun of motorists. The strip below was published in 1905.

**①** Louis Renault and his mechanic Szisz waiting to start one of the stages of the Paris–Madrid race, after being escorted through a town by a cyclist. Louis drove very fast and was first to arrive at Bordeaux. He did not know that his brother Marcel had met with a bad accident.

**②** Marcel Renault before the start of the race. His car, a Renault of course, was almost identical to the one Louis was driving. Marcel never reached Bordeaux. Blinded by the dust as he was passing another car, he did not see a right-angled bend ahead. He shot off the road and into a ditch.

**③** Marcel Renault's car lying mangled in the ditch into which it crashed. Marcel himself was unconscious when rescuers reached the wreck and he died the following day in hospital. When Louis was told of the tragedy in Bordeaux, he raced back to the spot as fast as he could.

**④** Another casualty of the race was an English driver called Lorraine Barrow who was driving a de Dietrich car. He is shown here waiting at the start. He has a strange expression on his face as if he had an idea that something was going to happen to him.

**⑤** Barrow's car was totally wrecked and his mechanic killed instantly when he crashed into a tree.
The accident was caused by a dog, which dashed out in front of the car. Barrow was badly injured in the crash and died several weeks later as a result of it.

**⑥** Women racing drivers were extremely rare at this time. The photograph shows Madame du Gast, a Frenchwoman, speeding on her way in the Paris–Madrid race. She was not among the first to reach Bordeaux because she stopped on the way to nurse some of those who were injured.

# The Best Car in the World

The Mercedes 60 of 1903 was probably the first car of the type now known as sports cars. It was low, open, light and fast.

The first Mercedes was built as a result of the influence an Austrian diplomat called Emil Jellinek had on the Daimler company. Jellinek had a talent for persuading rich people to buy expensive cars. He told Daimler that he wanted a new type of fast racing car with a new name. (He suggested Mercedes, the name of his 11-year-old daughter,

as a name that would sell well.) He promised that if the new car met with his approval he would order 36 of them to sell to his clients.

## A great success

The first Mercedes was completed in 1901, and Jellinek *did* approve. The next year he ordered a more powerful version – the 60 – which appeared in 1903. This car was so successful that for several years it was labelled "the best car in the world".

Unfortunately, Gottlieb Daimler did not live to see its success – he died in 1900.

## 1903 Mercedes

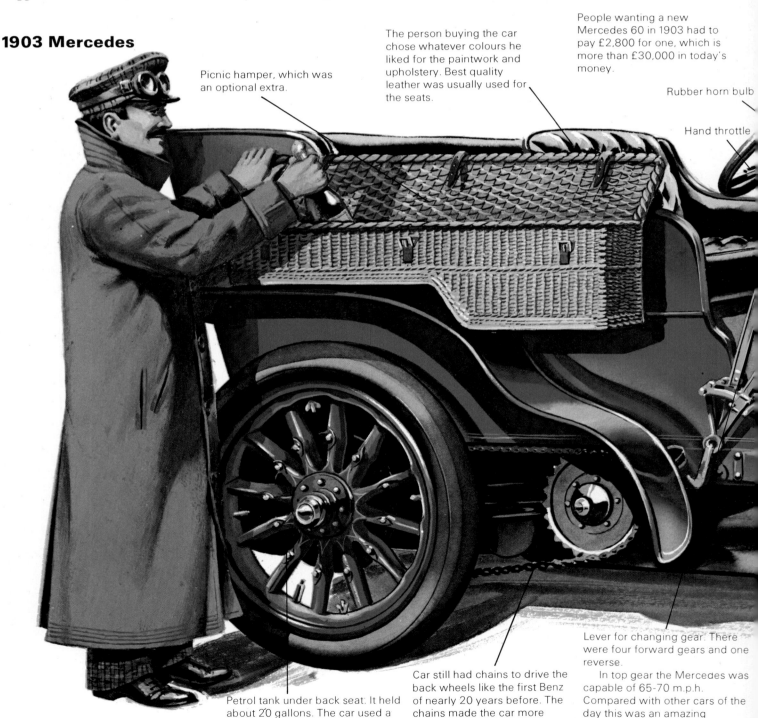

Picnic hamper, which was an optional extra.

The person buying the car chose whatever colours he liked for the paintwork and upholstery. Best quality leather was usually used for the seats.

People wanting a new Mercedes 60 in 1903 had to pay £2,800 for one, which is more than £30,000 in today's money.

Rubber horn bulb

Hand throttle

Petrol tank under back seat. It held about 20 gallons. The car used a gallon every 10–15 miles.

Car still had chains to drive the back wheels like the first Benz of nearly 20 years before. The chains made the car more noisy than it need have been.

Lever for changing gear. There were four forward gears and one reverse.
In top gear the Mercedes was capable of 65-70 m.p.h. Compared with other cars of the day this was an amazing performance.

▲ **The wreck of a Mercedes 60** in which famous
Polish racing driver Count Zborowski was killed in 1903.
Zborowski was obsessed by the Mercedes cars and liked
to drive very fast. He crashed to his death when his shirt
cuff caught on the hand throttle as he was turning a corner.

▲ **Count Louis Zborowski** followed in
his father's footsteps to become
another great racing driver. In the
1920s, he too was killed while driving

a Mercedes. At the time he was
wearing the same cuff links that his
father had been wearing when he
crashed to his death.

▶ **Mercedes Jellinek,** whose
name was given to the new
Daimler car of 1901. Her sister
Maja's name was used by the
Austrian Daimler company
in the same way.

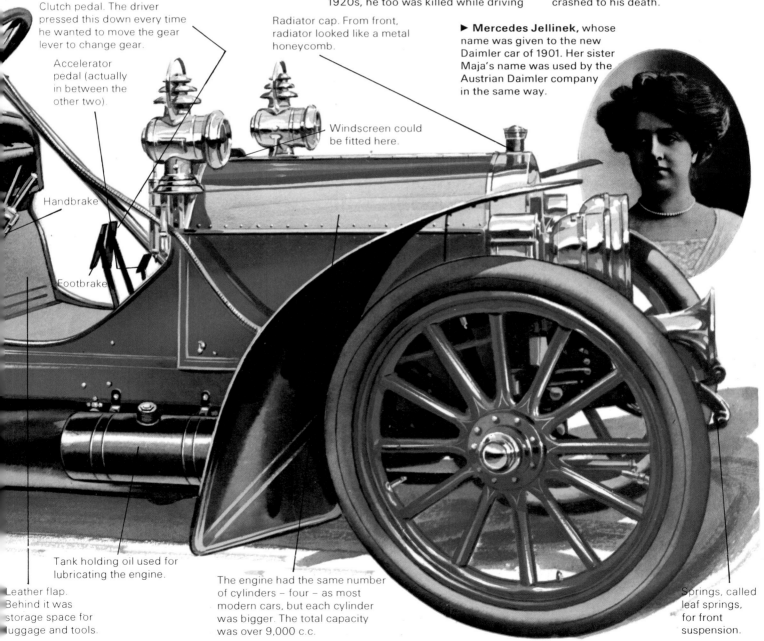

Clutch pedal. The driver
pressed this down every time
he wanted to move the gear
lever to change gear.

Radiator cap. From front,
radiator looked like a metal
honeycomb.

Accelerator
pedal (actually
in between the
other two).

Windscreen could
be fitted here.

Handbrake

Footbrake

Tank holding oil used for
lubricating the engine.

Leather flap.
Behind it was
storage space for
luggage and tools.

The engine had the same number
of cylinders – four – as most
modern cars, but each cylinder
was bigger. The total capacity
was over 9,000 c.c.

Springs, called
leaf springs,
for front
suspension.

# Preparing for a Run

Setting out in a motor car in the early days of motoring was a real adventure. Motorists were never quite sure what would happen on the way, or even if they would be able to get back. The sensible motorist made sure he prepared properly for every journey. That could mean several hours' work every time he wanted to go out.

Nearly every part of the car had to be cleaned, checked, oiled, greased or filled up. He had to make sure that he had enough tools, spares, petrol and oil to meet all emergencies. There were no breakdown trucks or garages along the way if anything went wrong. There were no petrol pumps either.

Petrol was bought in cans from local hardware stores.

It was windy and dusty travelling at 30–40 m.p.h. in an open car. Passengers covered themselves up as much as they could in long dust coats, hats, goggles and veils. These kept the dust out of their clothes and hair and kept them warm. If they were still cold, they took rugs and special footwarmers too.

If the weather was really cold, anti-freeze mixture would have to be made to stop the water in the radiator freezing up. A good mixture could be made at home from one part of methylated spirits, one part of glycerine and six parts of water. This, would stop freezing as long as the temperature stayed above −13°C. If it was colder than that, it was best to empty the radiator and not take the car out at all.

▲ **This particular car had a back entrance.** The seats were hard and not very comfortable.

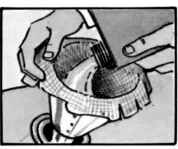

▲ **Dirt was kept out of the tank** by straining the petrol through a funnel lined with clean cloth.

▲ **Tyres were not very good.** They usually needed pumping up before a journey.

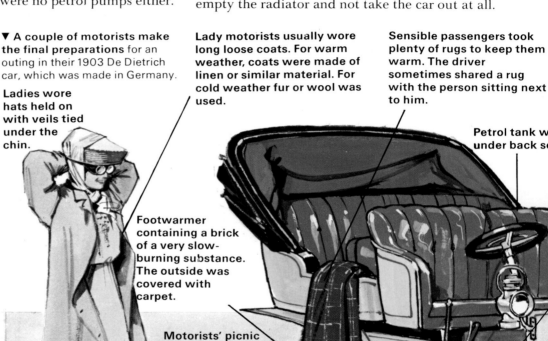

▼ **A couple of motorists make the final preparations** for an outing in their 1903 De Dietrich car, which was made in Germany.

**Ladies wore hats held on with veils tied under the chin.**

**Lady motorists usually wore long loose coats. For warm weather, coats were made of linen or similar material. For cold weather fur or wool was used.**

**Sensible passengers took plenty of rugs to keep them warm. The driver sometimes shared a rug with the person sitting next to him.**

**Petrol tank was under back seat.**

**Footwarmer containing a brick of a very slow-burning substance. The outside was covered with carpet.**

**Motorists' picnic hamper.**

**Pump**

**Spare tyres and inner tubes.**

**Driver's leather gauntlets.**

**Jack for lifting up the car while tyres were changed.**

**Patching equipment.**

**Lubricating oil**

**Water, often carried in an old petrol can.**

**Carbide for the acetylene lamps.**

**Petrol**

▲ **Motorists bought fuel for** their cars in two-gallon cans from local shops. Horse-drawn tankers were used by the oil companies for delivering supplies to the shops.

**Acetylene headlamps. These needed a lot of care as they blocked up easily. They needed filling with water and carbide before each trip. When burning they gave a good light, but were smelly.**

**Tools were sometimes supplied with the car. The toolbox was often placed on the running board.**

It was advisable to check the engine before setting out. Motorists had to be competent mechanics. They had to do most repairs themselves and manufacturers did not always provide a manual to help them.

**Goggles were necessary to protect the eyes from dust.**

**Tyre levers for easing tyres off the rims.**

**Special motorists' tool kits were made. There was a special place for each tool.**

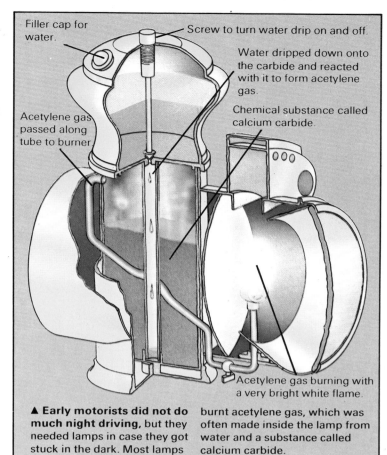

Filler cap for water.

Screw to turn water drip on and off.

Water dripped down onto the carbide and reacted with it to form acetylene gas.

Chemical substance called calcium carbide.

Acetylene gas passed along tube to burner

Acetylene gas burning with a very bright white flame.

▲ **Early motorists did not do much night driving,** but they needed lamps in case they got stuck in the dark. Most lamps burnt acetylene gas, which was often made inside the lamp from water and a substance called calcium carbide.

# Motoring fashions

▲ Lady's motoring veil.

▲ Gentleman's motoring helmet

▲ **A selection of the motoring clothes** advertised for sale during the early years of this century.

# How to Drive a Veteran Car

**There were no self-starters** on early cars. The driver had to turn the engine crankshaft by hand until the fuel started exploding the cylinders. In cold weather it was often necessary to put a teaspoonful of petrol into each cylinder to help start the engine. The choke has this effect on modern cars.

Ignition timing lever

▲ It was very important for all levers to be correctly positioned for starting the engine.

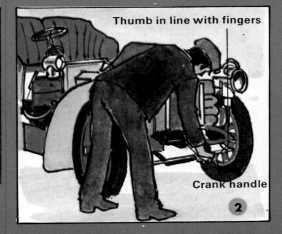

Thumb in line with fingers

Crank handle

◄ The crank handle was pushed in so as to engage it with the engine and then given a sharp pull upwards. If the engine backfired, the handle could jerk violently and perhaps break the driver's arm or thumb. So cranking had to be done very carefully.

# On the Road

It was unlikely that any motorist would be unfortunate enough to suffer all the mishaps shown here in one single journey. But he was sure to meet with some problem along the way, even if it was only a puncture. Punctures were very frequent because tyres were poor and roads were strewn with stones and horse-shoe nails. The pictures on these pages show some fairly common early motoring scenes.

The dust thrown up was a problem for motorists and anyone else who happened to be nearby.

Certain places became popular as resorts where motorists met. Notice the driver checking his watch. Men started using wristwatches because it was so difficult to extract a pocket watch from inside motoring clothes.

3 JOT

There were very few road signs, and maps were often inaccurate pencil sketches, so motorists sometimes became lost.

3 JOT

Throttle lever

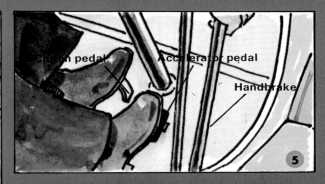

Clutch pedal  Accelerator pedal

Handbrake

▲ As soon as it started, the driver had to dash round to open the throttle so the engine did not stall.

▲ After climbing in, he put his left foot on the clutch pedal and pushed the gear lever forward into low gear.

▲ He moved his right foot down on the accelerator, took his left foot slowly off the clutch, gently released the handbrake and the car moved off.

Wheels were not detachable. The tyre had to be levered off with special tyre levers while the car was jacked up. A new or mended inner tube was stretched over the wheel and the outer cover replaced.

Narrow roads were a problem. Sometimes the motorist had to get out and ask cart drivers to move over so he could pass.

If it rained, the driver had to stop and get out to raise the hood, though this did not offer the passengers very much protection.

When the car broke down, the driver had to crawl underneath and see if he could find the cause of the trouble. Dust in the engine and overheating were common problems.

If the motorist could not mend the fault, he would often have to persuade a farmer to help out. Farmers usually charged for this service.

23

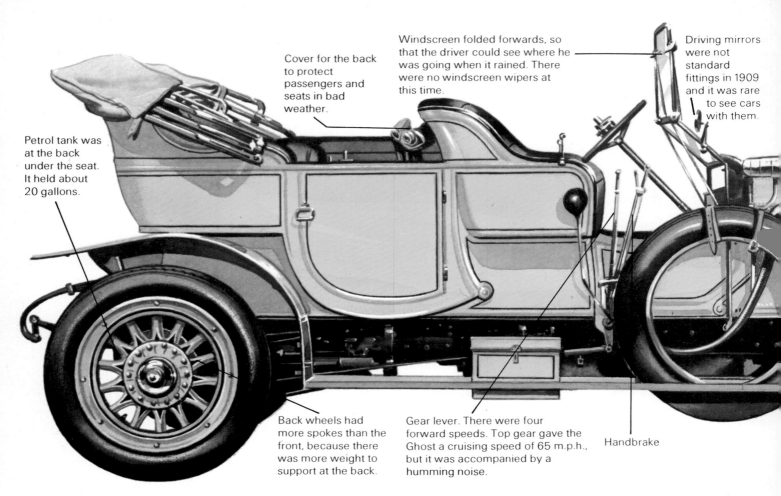

Cover for the back to protect passengers and seats in bad weather.

Windscreen folded forwards, so that the driver could see where he was going when it rained. There were no windscreen wipers at this time.

Driving mirrors were not standard fittings in 1909 and it was rare to see cars with them.

Petrol tank was at the back under the seat. It held about 20 gallons.

Back wheels had more spokes than the front, because there was more weight to support at the back.

Gear lever. There were four forward speeds. Top gear gave the Ghost a cruising speed of 65 m.p.h., but it was accompanied by a humming noise.

Handbrake

## Some of the models to choose from

▼ The cars shown here are just a small selection from those available during the first few years of this century.

1906 Renault in use as a London taxi. The car was tall enough for a man wearing a top hat to walk into without bending over.

Four-seater Sunbeam of 1904. Open cars of this type with hoods were called touring cars. Owners often drove them themselves.

1905 Dutch Spyker owned by actress Isabel Jay. It was a touring car, with a hood similar to that on the Sunbeam. Spyker was one of the first companies to make cars with six-cylinder engines, though this particular model had only four.

Windscreens were not allowed on taxis until windscreen wipers came into use.

# Rolls-Royce and Others

By 1906, the motor car was no longer an experiment. It really worked. People had realized that it was more than just a passing hobby for those who had plenty of money and time to spare. Car makers were now concentrating on making their products go *well*, instead of just making them go.

Motorists were growing in number and a lot of them wanted something other than a machine that gave them the thrill of speed and a mechanical puzzle to solve. They wanted a comfortable and reliable method of transport that did not force them to wear heavy clothes and goggles.

## Royal motorists

By this time also, motoring had stopped being shocking. It had become very respectable to own and drive a motor car – even royalty did it. Kaiser Wilhelm II of Germany owned a 60 h.p. Mercedes. King Alfonso XIII of Spain and Edward, Prince of Wales, later King Edward VII of England, were both enthusiastic motorists. It no longer mattered if car owners were not mechanically inclined. They could hire a chauffeur to look after that side of motoring for them.

A wide variety of cars was available to choose from. There was something to suit everyone's taste – as long as they were rich. Some of them are shown on these two pages.

▼ **Rolls-Royce Silver Ghost** of 1909. The Rolls-Royce company was started by two car enthusiasts who were looking for a perfect car. Henry Royce, an engineer, built the cars. Charles Rolls, a rich aristocrat, supplied the money and sold the cars.

The name "Silver Ghost" came from the first model that was made. It had shiny aluminium bodywork with silver-plated accessories, and was very quiet compared with other cars of the time. Other Silver Ghosts were finished to customers' requirements.

Engine had six cylinders and a capacity of seven litres.

Mascot, sometimes called the "Spirit of Ecstasy". It was not designed until 1911, so this car was not fitted with one when it was built.

Italian Fiat made around 1901. Fiat had started making cars two years earlier. This model was one of the smallest cars available at the time. It could hold four at a squeeze – there was a seat behind the hood.

Model A Cadillac of 1903. Its engine was mounted under the floor and had just one cylinder. Ladies tried to climb in without showing their ankles.

## Cigarette cards

◀ **1904 Standard** made in Britain. It had a one-cylinder engine which was placed under the front floor boards.

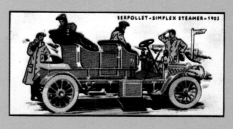

◀ **Serpollet-Simplex steam car** made in France in 1903. Compared with internal combustion engined cars, steamers were very quiet. The boiler was at the back.

◀ **Electric cab,** called an Electromobile. These were popular in towns. Their speed was about 15 m.p.h. and their batteries needed recharging about every 25 miles.

# Running Costs

If a person owned a carriage and horses in the 19th century, he was either a very successful business or professional man, or had inherited enough money not to have to work for his living at all. No-one else could possibly afford the expense of keeping at the very least two horses, a coachman and a groom. A carriage alone cost around £200 at a time when a skilled workman was keeping his family on wages of less than £100 a year.

Nevertheless, people usually kept a carriage if they could possibly afford to because of the prestige it involved.

The costs given on these pages are the actual prices a buyer had to pay at the beginning of this century. You can work out approximate equivalent amounts in today's money by multiplying them by 12. Note that these equivalent amounts are *not* the prices of similar articles in the shops today.

## Running a motor car

In the early 1900s cars were generally more expensive to buy than similarly sized horse-drawn carriages, but they were cheaper to run. For one thing, a car did not need "feeding" when it was not in use like a horse did. Contemporary estimates put the running costs of a pony and trap at 6d a mile and a small car at 4d a mile (equivalent to 27p and 18p in today's money). The cheapest car cost £200, however, and that put motoring totally beyond the reach of most people.

In America, things were a bit different. American cars were generally smaller, simpler and cheaper than those built in Europe, where manufacturers were concerned with quality and luxury. Petrol was cheaper too because it was found there.

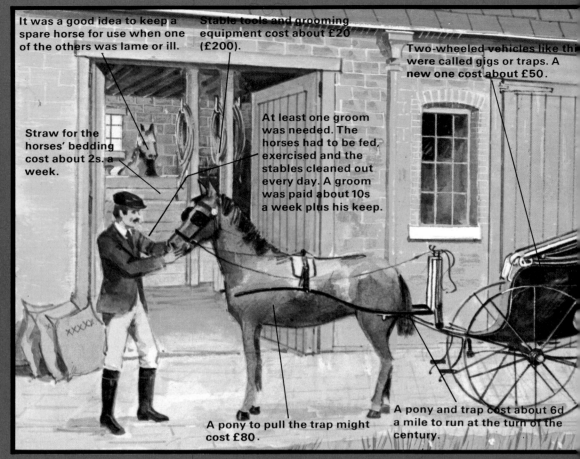

It was a good idea to keep a spare horse for use when one of the others was lame or ill.

Stable tools and grooming equipment cost about £20 (£200).

Two-wheeled vehicles like this were called gigs or traps. A new one cost about £50.

Straw for the horses' bedding cost about 2s. a week.

At least one groom was needed. The horses had to be fed, exercised and the stables cleaned out every day. A groom was paid about 10s a week plus his keep.

A pony to pull the trap might cost £80.

A pony and trap cost about 6d a mile to run at the turn of the century.

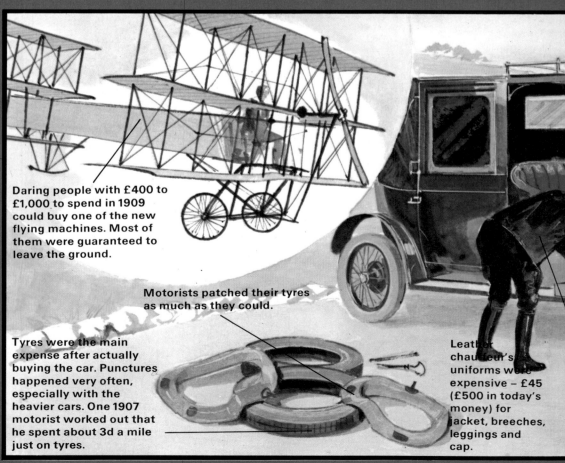

Daring people with £400 to £1,000 to spend in 1909 could buy one of the new flying machines. Most of them were guaranteed to leave the ground.

Motorists patched their tyres as much as they could.

Tyres were the main expense after actually buying the car. Punctures happened very often, especially with the heavier cars. One 1907 motorist worked out that he spent about 3d a mile just on tyres.

Leather chauffeur's uniforms were expensive – £45 (£500 in today's money) for jacket, breeches, leggings and cap.

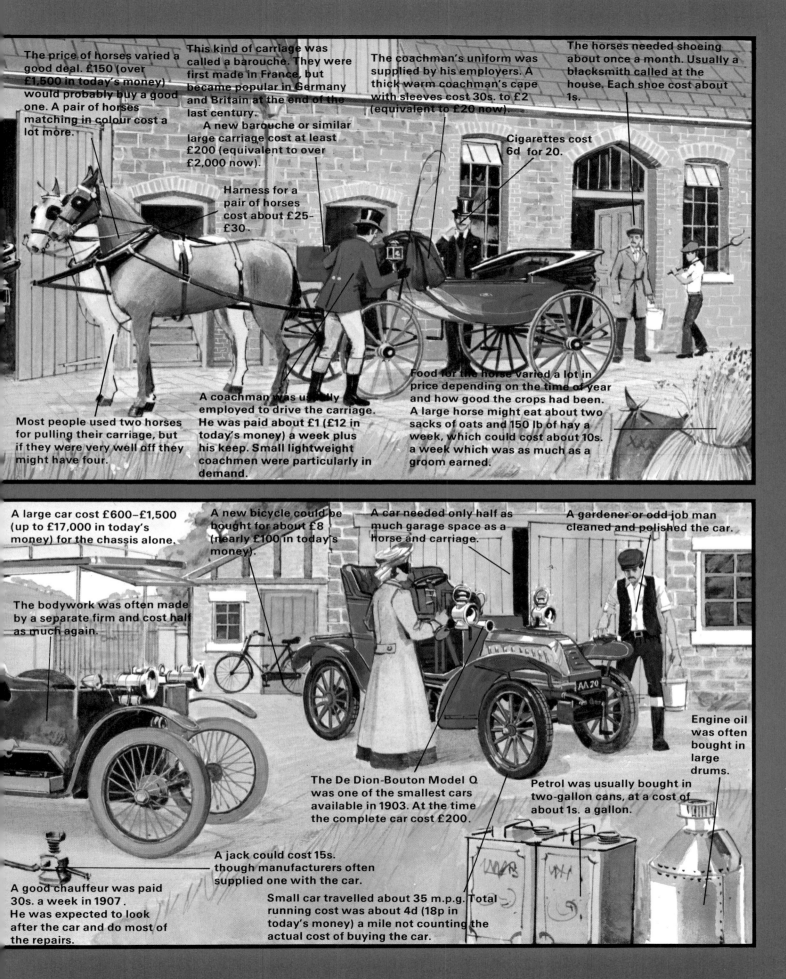

The price of horses varied a good deal. £150 (over £1,500 in today's money) would probably buy a good one. A pair of horses matching in colour cost a lot more.

This kind of carriage was called a barouche. They were first made in France, but became popular in Germany and Britain at the end of the last century.
    A new barouche or similar large carriage cost at least £200 (equivalent to over £2,000 now).

The coachman's uniform was supplied by his employers. A thick warm coachman's cape with sleeves cost 30s. to £2 (equivalent to £20 now).

The horses needed shoeing about once a month. Usually a blacksmith called at the house. Each shoe cost about 1s.

Cigarettes cost 6d for 20.

Harness for a pair of horses cost about £25-£30.

Most people used two horses for pulling their carriage, but if they were very well off they might have four.

A coachman was usually employed to drive the carriage. He was paid about £1 (£12 in today's money) a week plus his keep. Small lightweight coachmen were particularly in demand.

Food for the horse varied a lot in price depending on the time of year and how good the crops had been. A large horse might eat about two sacks of oats and 150 lb of hay a week, which could cost about 10s. a week which was as much as a groom earned.

A large car cost £600–£1,500 (up to £17,000 in today's money) for the chassis alone.

A new bicycle could be bought for about £8 (nearly £100 in today's money).

A car needed only half as much garage space as a horse and carriage.

A gardener or odd job man cleaned and polished the car.

The bodywork was often made by a separate firm and cost half as much again.

The De Dion-Bouton Model Q was one of the smallest cars available in 1903. At the time the complete car cost £200.

Engine oil was often bought in large drums.

Petrol was usually bought in two-gallon cans, at a cost of about 1s. a gallon.

A jack could cost 15s. though manufacturers often supplied one with the car.

A good chauffeur was paid 30s. a week in 1907. He was expected to look after the car and do most of the repairs.

Small car travelled about 35 m.p.g. Total running cost was about 4d (18p in today's money) a mile not counting the actual cost of buying the car.

# Optional Extras

Some of the optional extras for early motorists are now essential standard fittings – like headlamps, windscreens, horns, speedometers, rear-view mirrors and bumper bars. Others were decorative but not very useful, like silver flower vases. In fact, anything that was not actually part of the bodywork was sold separately at extra cost.

The car accessories on these pages are just some of the things that could be found in catalogues printed during the first ten years of this century.

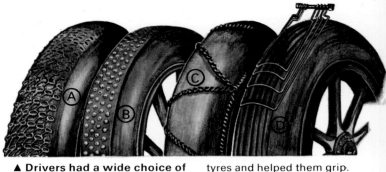

▲ **Drivers had a wide choice of tyres** and devices to prevent puncturing and skidding.
**A.** Tyres were smooth for a long time. This was an early type with tread. **B.** Metal studs protected tyres and helped them grip.
**C.** Chains were used to stop skidding in bad weather.
**D.** A "nail-catcher" knocked out nails and stones before they were pressed in.

▶ **A spare-tyre case** protected the tyres from sun, wind and rain in the days before cars had any luggage space inside them. The manufacturer of this one had the clever idea of combining it with a hat box, so that the space in the centre of the tyre was not wasted.

▲ **Most countries made laws compelling motorists** to have some way of warning people of their approach. A horn with a rubber bulb was most common. This snake's head horn was one of the most expensive.

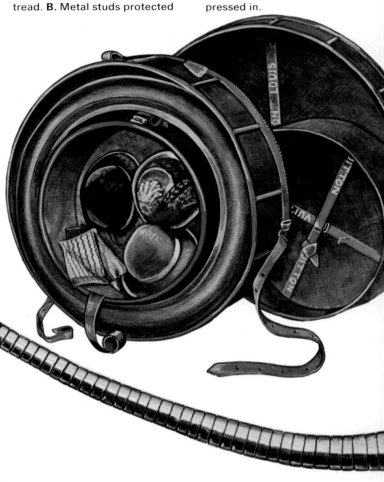

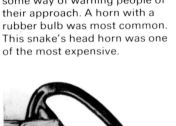

◀ **A mouth siren** strapped to the driver's wrist could also be used to warn people that a car was coming. Some motorists had trouble making their horns heard over the noise of the engine, so it was perhaps a good idea to have a siren as well.

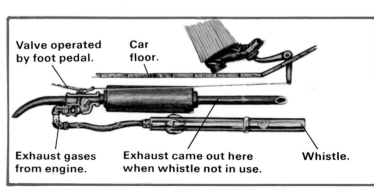

Valve operated by foot pedal.    Car floor.

Exhaust gases from engine.    Exhaust came out here when whistle not in use.    Whistle.

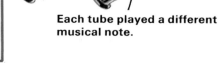

Each tube played a different musical note.

Cardboard records were put in here.

▲ **An ingenious way of signalling a car's approach** was a whistle attached to the exhaust pipe. A pedal operated a valve which diverted the exhaust gas through the whistle.

▲ **This horn played a tune.** It came supplied with perforated cardboard records which made it play different tunes. Without a record, all four tubes sounded their notes together.

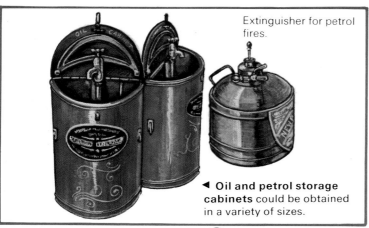

Extinguisher for petrol fires.

◄ **Oil and petrol storage cabinets** could be obtained in a variety of sizes.

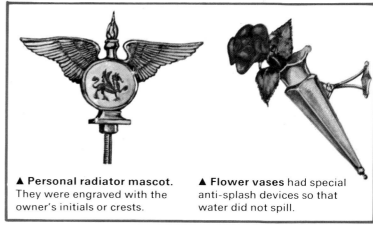

▲ **Personal radiator mascot.** They were engraved with the owner's initials or crests.

▲ **Flower vases** had special anti-splash devices so that water did not spill.

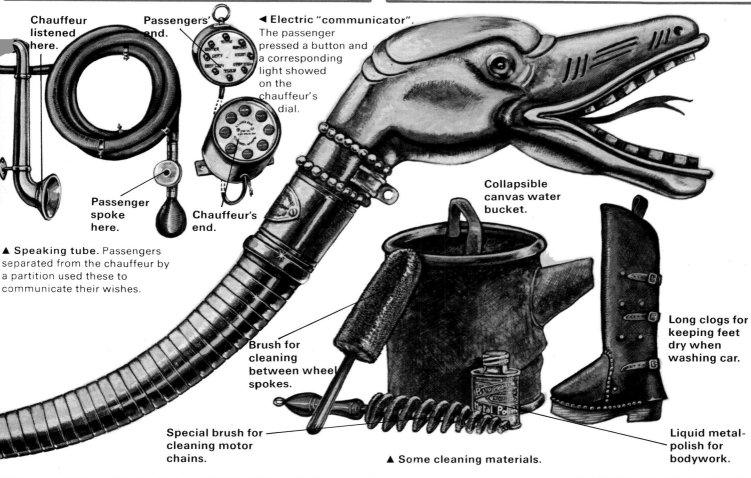

**Chauffeur listened here.**

**Passengers' end.**

◄ **Electric "communicator".** The passenger pressed a button and a corresponding light showed on the chauffeur's dial.

**Passenger spoke here.**

**Chauffeur's end.**

▲ **Speaking tube.** Passengers separated from the chauffeur by a partition used these to communicate their wishes.

**Collapsible canvas water bucket.**

**Brush for cleaning between wheel spokes.**

**Special brush for cleaning motor chains.**

▲ **Some cleaning materials.**

**Long clogs for keeping feet dry when washing car.**

**Liquid metal-polish for bodywork.**

▲ **Advertisement for windshields** in an American magazine of 1910.

▲ **A device for reducing the injuries** of pedestrians who were run down by cars.

PROTECT YOUR CAR *against theft*
Locks may be picked or jimmied. Cars may be stolen in spite of them
**BUT** NO THIEF EVER ATTEMPTED TO STEAL A CAR WITH A MAN AT THE WHEEL
Bosco's **COLLAPSIBLE RUBBER DRIVER**

▲ **Blow-up rubber "thief-repeller"** to frighten away car thieves.

▲ **Rubber storm apron** with holes in it for peoples' heads to fit through.

# Exploring the Limits

An 18th century English writer said he believed 20 m.p.h. to be the fastest anyone could travel and still be able to breathe. Railway trains proved how wrong he was. The first official land speed record run was recorded in 1898. A Frenchman called the Comte de Chasseloup-Laubat buzzed along at just under 40 m.p.h. in an electric car. It was probably a very dull event.

This record lasted a month. It was broken by a Belgian called Camille Jenatzy, who later became a famous racing driver and gained the nickname "Red Devil" because of the colour of his beard. Jenatzy and Chasseloup-Laubat broke each other's records several times in that year. The determined Jenatzy eventually ordered a special car to be made. He called it *La Jamais Contente* (which means "never

satisfied"). Its very large electric batteries were capable of an enormous, though short-lived, burst of power.

On April 1, 1899, Jenatzy covered the specially measured kilometre of road very quickly indeed – but the time-keepers were not ready for him. A few weeks later he tried again. This time he officially reached a speed of just over 100 kilometres an hour (about 65 m.p.h.). Hundreds of record-breaking attempts have been made since Jenatzy's time, and in some very strange-looking vehicles. In 1970, the world land speed record was raised to an incredible 631 m.p.h. by the American, Gary Gabelich in Blue Flame.

The limits of endurance of drivers and vehicles are not so easily measured. One of the greatest tests must have been the Peking to Paris motor race held in 1907. The cars were shipped out from Paris to Peking and left to find their way back again overland. It would be a fairly daunting task today. In 1907 it was considered quite crazy.

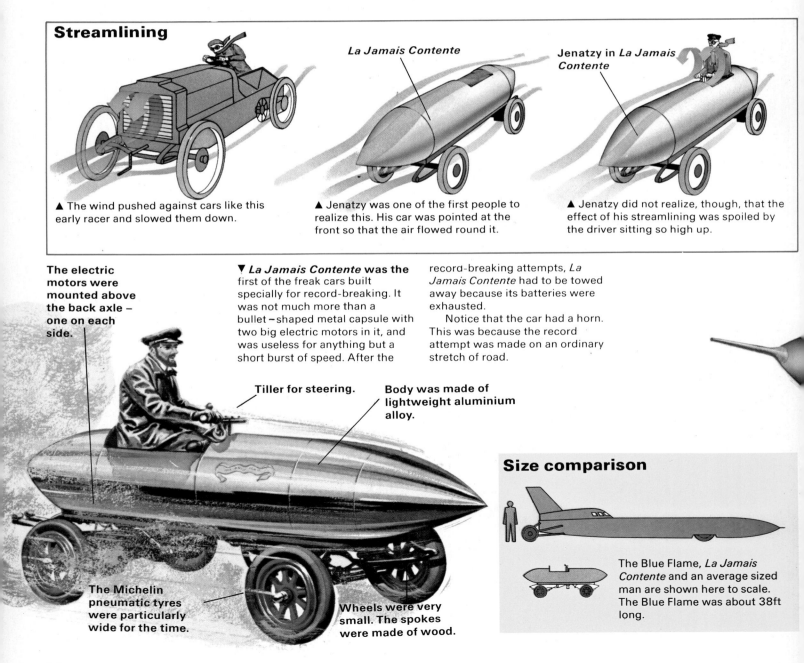

**Streamlining**

▲ The wind pushed against cars like this early racer and slowed them down.

*La Jamais Contente*

▲ Jenatzy was one of the first people to realize this. His car was pointed at the front so that the air flowed round it.

Jenatzy in *La Jamais Contente*

▲ Jenatzy did not realize, though, that the effect of his streamlining was spoiled by the driver sitting so high up.

**The electric motors were mounted above the back axle – one on each side.**

▼ *La Jamais Contente* was the first of the freak cars built specially for record-breaking. It was not much more than a bullet –shaped metal capsule with two big electric motors in it, and was useless for anything but a short burst of speed. After the

record-breaking attempts, *La Jamais Contente* had to be towed away because its batteries were exhausted.

Notice that the car had a horn. This was because the record attempt was made on an ordinary stretch of road.

**Tiller for steering.**

**Body was made of lightweight aluminium alloy.**

**The Michelin pneumatic tyres were particularly wide for the time.**

**Wheels were very small. The spokes were made of wood.**

**Size comparison**

The Blue Flame, *La Jamais Contente* and an average sized man are shown here to scale. The Blue Flame was about 38ft long.

**1** In June 1907, five cars waited to start on the most adventurous race ever to take place. They were going to drive half way across the world from Peking in China to Paris in France.

**2** They had little idea of what they would meet on the way. The first few hundred miles were through terrible mountainous areas where there were no roads at all.

**3** The scenery changed when they crossed over the frontiers of Mongolia and into the Gobi desert. Two of the contestants were lucky enough to find a well to bathe in.

**4** Prince Borghese, the only Italian in the race, took the lead almost immediately. His country's flag is seen here flying over his camp in the Gobi desert.

**5** Mud was one of the thousands of obstacles the cars had to face. Here, a De Dion Bouton, one of the French cars in the race, is being rescued by horses.

**6** Amazingly, four out of the five cars survived the trial. Prince Borghese in his Itala is shown here arriving in Paris. He was almost three weeks ahead of the others.

Cockpit where driver sat.

Parachutes to help stop the Blue Flame were housed above the jet nozzles. On some of the test runs, the parachute cords caught fire. Without them the Blue Flame took 12 miles to stop.

It was called the Blue Flame because the sponsors were the Natural Gas Corporation of America, and natural gas burns with a blue flame.

The Blue Flame had a motor which burnt liquid fuel. Liquified natural gas and hydrogen peroxide were used as fuel and were kept in separate pressurized tanks. The mixing of the two liquids provided the tremendous explosive force which drove the vehicle along.

▲ The Blue Flame which broke the world land speed record in 1970. It was rocket-powered and looked more like an aeroplane without wings than a car. But it was perhaps not as unlike *La Jamais Contente* in appearance as might be expected.

The driver was Gary Gabelich, an American dragster racer.

31

# How a Car Works

Motor cars, even the very early ones, are very complicated machines. Finding out exactly how they work in every detail needs a lot of careful study. But the general ideas behind the workings of a car are quite simple.

The most important part is the engine, which provides the power to make the car move. Nearly all modern cars have, in principle, the same type of engine as the one Benz used in his first car. Because the fuel burns *inside*, it is called the internal combustion engine. It works in the following way. Exploding fuel forces a piston to move in a cylinder.

Benz's engine had just one cylinder. Modern cars have four, six or even more, firing one after another, but basically they work in the same way.

Then there is the clutch. When the clutch is disengaged, the engine is not directly connected to the wheels. So the engine can be going without the car moving along.

The other important part is the gearbox. This contains a number of different sized cogs joined together in groups on short rods. The car's speed can be changed without the engine speed changing by making different combinations of cogs mesh together.

The pictures on this page will help you understand how a car works.

## The engine

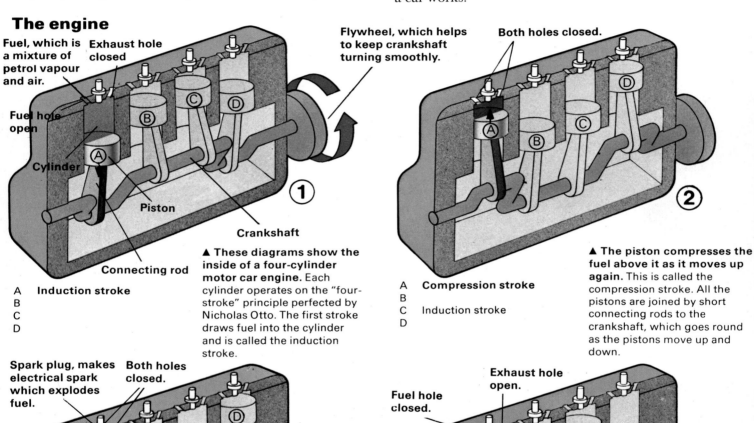

**Fuel, which is a mixture of petrol vapour and air.**
**Exhaust hole closed**
**Flywheel, which helps to keep crankshaft turning smoothly.**
**Fuel hole open**
**Cylinder**
**Connecting rod**
**Piston**
**Crankshaft**

① 
A **Induction stroke**
B
C
D

▲ **These diagrams show the inside of a four-cylinder motor car engine.** Each cylinder operates on the "four-stroke" principle perfected by Nicholas Otto. The first stroke draws fuel into the cylinder and is called the induction stroke.

**Both holes closed.**

②
A **Compression stroke**
B
C **Induction stroke**
D

▲ **The piston compresses the fuel above it as it moves up again.** This is called the compression stroke. All the pistons are joined by short connecting rods to the crankshaft, which goes round as the pistons move up and down.

**Spark plug, makes electrical spark which explodes fuel.**
**Both holes closed.**

③
A **Power stroke**
B
C Compression stroke
D Induction stroke

▲ **At the top of the compression stroke,** an electric spark makes the fuel explode. The force of the explosion pushes the piston down the cylinder in the power stroke. This is the only stroke in which power is actually generated.

**Fuel hole closed.**
**Exhaust hole open.**

④
A **Exhaust stroke**
B Induction stroke
C Power stroke
D Compression stroke

▲ **The fourth stroke pushes the exhaust gases out of the cylinder.** At the top of this stroke, the exhaust outlet hole closes and the fuel inlet hole opens ready for another induction stroke. The fuel and exhaust holes are opened and closed at the correct times by valves.

Discs apart – clutch disengaged.

Discs pressed together – clutch engaged.

## The clutch

▲ **Very simply, a clutch is two discs.** The engine drives one disc all the time. The other one goes round only when it is pressed close to the first one. The clutch is then "engaged"

## The gears

▶ **A small cog is driven** by the engine. Its teeth mesh with another cog twice its size, making the larger cog go round too. But, because it is twice as big, it only turns once for every two turns of the little cog.

By using these two cogs, the driving speed has been halved. The engine still has the same power, however, so this arrangement of gears can help a car climb hills.

▶ **When the large cog is driven** by the engine the opposite happens. The speed is doubled because the small cog goes round twice for one turn of the large cog. This arrangement of gears is useful for speeding along flat stretches of road.

A real gearbox contains lots of cogs of different sizes, but basically they all work in the same way as the ones in these diagrams.

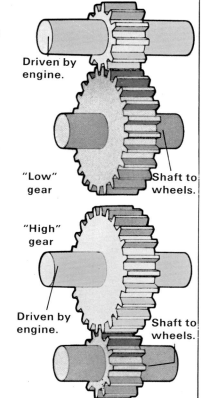

Driven by engine.

"Low" gear

Shaft to wheels.

"High" gear

Driven by engine.

Shaft to wheels.

## The differential

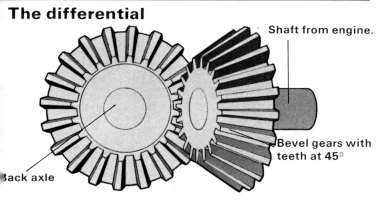

Shaft from engine.

Bevel gears with teeth at 45°

Back axle

▲ **In most cars, the engine drives a long shaft** which runs from the front of the car to the back. Somehow, the motion of this shaft must be turned through a right-angle so that it drives the back axle. Two special cogs, called bevel gears, are used for this.

The differential also includes other cogs (not shown here) which allow the two back wheels to go at different speeds when turning corners.

## Where all the parts belong

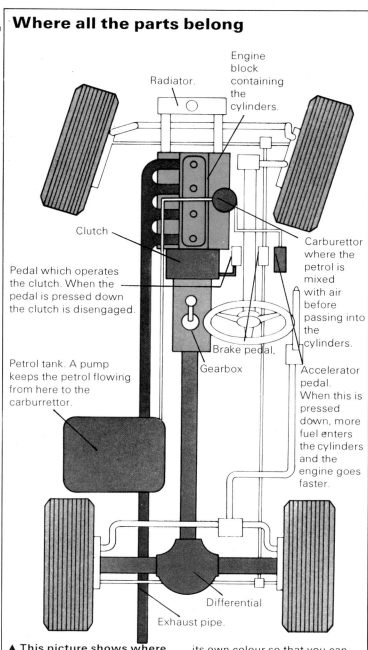

Radiator.

Engine block containing the cylinders.

Clutch

Pedal which operates the clutch. When the pedal is pressed down the clutch is disengaged.

Petrol tank. A pump keeps the petrol flowing from here to the carburrettor.

Brake pedal,

Gearbox

Carburettor where the petrol is mixed with air before passing into the cylinders.

Accelerator pedal. When this is pressed down, more fuel enters the cylinders and the engine goes faster.

Differential

Exhaust pipe.

▲ **This picture shows where all the separate parts described on these pages fit into a car.** Each part has its own colour so that you can find it easily. Obviously not all cars are like this – some have engines at the back for instance.

## Some car terms explained

**Engine size.** The volume of the cylinder space above the piston when the piston is at its lowest position, multiplied by the number of cylinders. It is usually given in cubic centimetres or litres.

**Revs per minute.** The number of times the flywheel goes round in one minute.

**Transmission.** The way in which power is transferred from the engine to the wheels. In this car, transmission is by shaft. Early cars often had belt or chain transmission.

**Gear ratio.** The relative sizes of the cogs used for a particular gear. For example, a cog with 50 teeth meshing with one with 40 teeth gives a ratio of $\frac{50}{40}$ or 1.25:1.

# Grand Prix and Indianapolis

The French Grand Prix, perhaps the greatest of all sports car races, was first held in 1906. The only big international race before this was the Gordon Bennett Cup. Mr Bennett, owner of the *New York Herald* newspaper, had organized and financed a race named after himself in 1900. Each country was allowed to enter a team of three cars. The next year's Gordon Bennett race was then organized in the winner's country.

After six of these races, the French decided that they produced far too many cars to be restricted to three. They withdrew and organized their own race – the French Grand Prix – in which the only restriction was that all cars had to weigh less than 1,000 kilograms.

By this time, cars were beginning to be designed specially for racing. The early racers were no more than modified versions of the cars on sale to the public. Manufacturers spent large sums of money on developing special cars. To make sure it was worthwhile, they engaged professional drivers to race them.

The year following the first Grand Prix saw the beginning of motor racing on tracks specially built for the purpose. This was the year in which the Brooklands track was opened in England. The track was 2¾ miles long and had banked corners which could be taken at higher speeds than flat ones. It cost £150,000 to build, a staggering amount of money in 1907. Two years later, in 1909, the famous Indianapolis race track was built in America.

▲ **To make cars go faster,** designers put bigger and bigger engines in them. They ended up with giant cars like this Fiat which had cylinders the size of dustbins. After a while, a limit was put on engine sizes in most race rules.

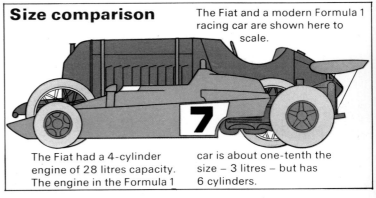

**Size comparison** The Fiat and a modern Formula 1 racing car are shown here to scale.

The Fiat had a 4-cylinder engine of 28 litres capacity. The engine in the Formula 1 car is about one-tenth the size – 3 litres – but has 6 cylinders.

**Mechanic kept his body well down in the car to lessen the wind resistance.**

**Rider-mechanics were banned in 1925 because too many of them had been killed in accidents.**

**Changing tyres without detachable rims.**

▶ **The winner of the first French Grand Prix** was the Hungarian driver, Szisz, who had been Louis Renault's mechanic in the 1903 Paris to Madrid race.

The drivers had to do 12 laps of a 64-mile triangular course near Le Mans in France. They had two days, but the cars were locked up overnight.

Szisz's success was partly due to new detachable rims invented by Michelin. While other drivers were scraping the remains of old tyres from their fixed wheel rims, Szisz had undone 12 nuts, removed his wheel rim and fitted another.

**Petrol tank was behind seats. One of the mechanic's jobs was to operate a hand pump which pumped the petrol to the engine.**

**The Grand Prix cars had right-hand drive because the races were all run in a clockwise direction.**

**Crank handle held in place with a strap while car was moving.**

**Car was a Renault with a four-cylinder, 12 litre engine.**

**Dust had been a terrible problem for drivers in previous races, so tar was laid on this course. But it was very hot weather and the tar melted. The hot liquid tar ruined tyres and burnt drivers' faces.** Szisz was burnt by hot tar and had to be led away at the end of the race with a handkerchief over his face.

**Radiator**

# The Indianapolis track

▼ **Cars revving up at the start** of one of the first races on the Indianapolis track – the 100-mile race of 1909.

The track was not very popular at first. Its surface was poor and began to break up almost immediately, causing several deaths. It was decided to re-surface it with bricks and hold just one long race a year. The race was to be 200 laps of the 2½-mile rectangular circuit, and the prize money an amazing $25,000.

The first Indianapolis 500, as it became known, was held in 1911.

▲ **The first Indianapolis 500** race was won by an American, called Ray Harroun in a yellow Marmon called a Wasp.

Harroun claimed that the car had never been flat out all the way. He drove the non-stop 500 miles at an average speed of 74½ m.p.h. Though fast at the time, this is less than half the speed averaged by today's 500 drivers.

Harroun's Marmon was the only single-seater to take part in the race. As he had no mechanic to check what was coming up behind him, Harroun had a driving mirror fitted to the car. It is thought to have been the first racing car to have a mirror.

The car was called "Wasp" because of its pointed tail, not because of its colour.

# Ford and the Model T

Building cars was slow work at the beginning of this century. Each one was built separately by hand. Parts were not standard – they were made individually, or in small numbers, as they were needed. The end result was often a fine piece of workmanship, but it was expensive.

If cars could be made more quickly, they could be cheaper. If they were cheaper, more would be sold. Henry Ford was the first person to put this into practice. In 1913 he succeeded in cutting the time for making a complete chassis from 12½ hours to 1½ hours.

## From pigs to cars

Ford did not invent the assembly line. It had been used in various food factories quite a long time before. Around 1870, a meat-packing factory in the American city of Cincinnatti (sometimes called Porkopolis because of the number of pigs killed there) was using an overhead line to move the dead pigs from one worker to another. Each worker stood in one place and made his particular cut as the pigs came past him.

The principle that Ford applied to car manufacturing was the same – take the work to the worker rather than the other way round. To save even more time, all the work was placed at waist level so that the men did not have to bend down.

## A very simple car

Ford designed a car with the assembly line in mind. It was as simple as could be, and was made up of as few separate parts as possible. He then divided its assembly up into a lot of small simple operations. Each of these could be performed by one man. The result was the Ford Model T – and he made millions of them.

## Inside a Model T

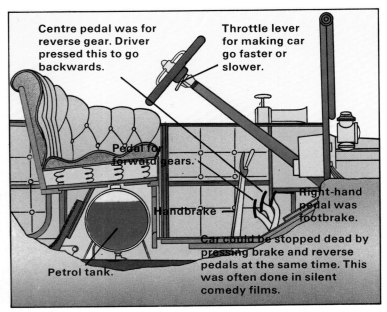

Centre pedal was for reverse gear. Driver pressed this to go backwards.

Throttle lever for making car go faster or slower.

Pedal for forward gears.

Handbrake

Right-hand pedal was footbrake.

Car could be stopped dead by pressing brake and reverse pedals at the same time. This was often done in silent comedy films.

Petrol tank.

▶ The first assembly line cars were made at the Ford factory in Michigan in America in 1913. The factory building was not big enough for the whole process to be completed inside, so final assembly of bodies and chassis was done outside.

By 1925, one Model T was being completed every ten seconds at the Michigan factory.

The finished Model T was very basic, with no extras whatsoever. In later years, a large accessory industry grew up just to supply Model T owners with little extras for their cars.

The four cylinders of the engine were cast together out of one piece of metal, instead of each one being made separately and fitted together afterwards.

By 1917, the price of a Model T had dropped from £250 to £130.

Very few cars had the steering wheel on the left-hand side before the Model T.

◀ Driving a Model T was completely different from driving any other car of the time (or indeed any other car since). Supposedly it was so easy that anyone could do it.

In an emergency the car could be slowed down by stepping on any of the three pedals. So it did not matter if the driver made a mistake.

It was not a very comfortable car to ride in, but it went well. Driving across fields was no trouble. Top speed was about 40 m.p.h., but it was rather noisy.

By 1927, a dozen variations of the Model T were available. All were basically the same and all came off the assembly lines. Here are some of them.

Light van – for deliveries. Price in 1927 : £122.

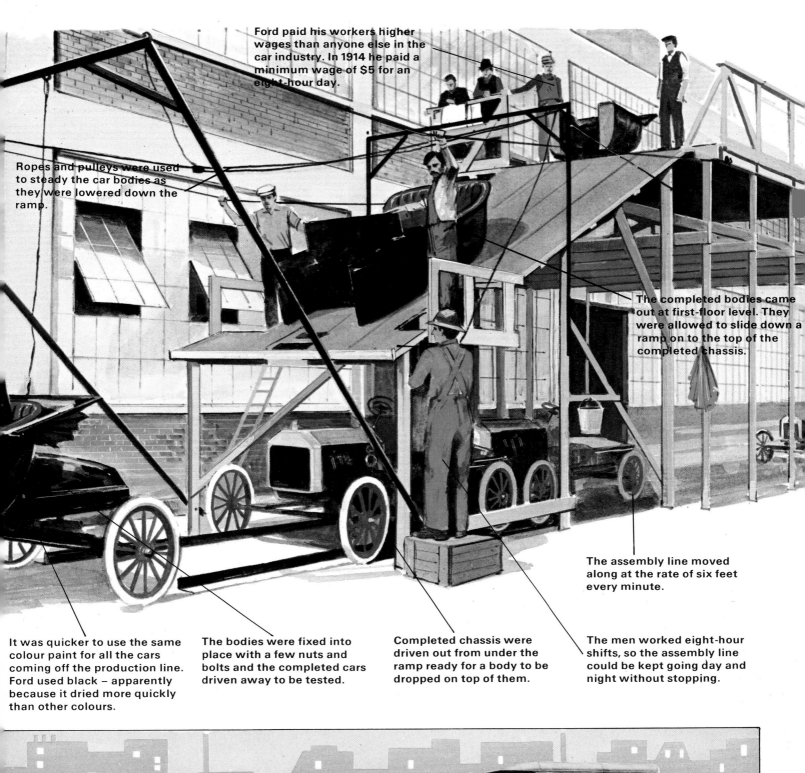

Ford paid his workers higher wages than anyone else in the car industry. In 1914 he paid a minimum wage of $5 for an eight-hour day.

Ropes and pulleys were used to steady the car bodies as they were lowered down the ramp.

The completed bodies came out at first-floor level. They were allowed to slide down a ramp on to the top of the completed chassis.

It was quicker to use the same colour paint for all the cars coming off the production line. Ford used black – apparently because it dried more quickly than other colours.

The bodies were fixed into place with a few nuts and bolts and the completed cars driven away to be tested.

Completed chassis were driven out from under the ramp ready for a body to be dropped on top of them.

The assembly line moved along at the rate of six feet every minute.

The men worked eight-hour shifts, so the assembly line could be kept going day and night without stopping.

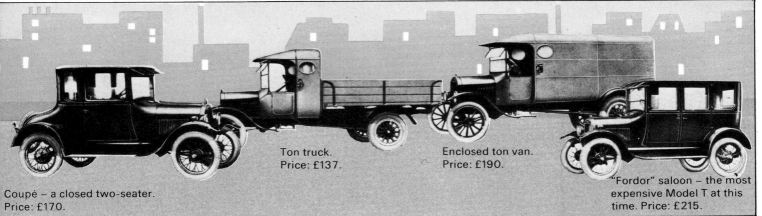

Coupé – a closed two-seater. Price: £170.

Ton truck. Price: £137.

Enclosed ton van. Price: £190.

"Fordor" saloon – the most expensive Model T at this time. Price: £215.

## After the war

The First World War, which started in 1914, demonstrated how very useful motor vehicles could be. It was also responsible for a certain amount of levelling out of money and class differences between people. Ordinary people became accustomed to using cars in the course of their wartime jobs. Naturally they wanted them afterwards too.

A number of firms started making cars after the war. Some had set up factories to make armaments and, when the war ended, turned their suddenly idle machinery to making cars. One of these was Citroën, who had been making explosive shells. Many of them followed in Ford's footsteps and produced thousands of small cheap cars – which was just what the new motorists wanted.

▲ **Lloyd was not a particularly well-known make of car,** but this one was sturdy enough to survive a game-hunting expedition in the East African jungle. Notice the metal studs on the tyres. These protected the tyres and helped them grip.

▲ **Family picnics were popular** among the new motoring public. This group was photographed at the Brooklands motor racing track in England during the Easter holiday of 1923.

▲ **Petrol stations** became a common sight during the 1920s – and not only in Europe and America. This photograph was taken in the town of Klang in Malaya.

▲ **Putting oil into the engine** was apparently so easy that ladies could do it in their best clothes. The car is a large 1920s Fiat.

▶ **A lady checks the oil level** on the dipstick (a recent invention) in her 1926 Renault.

▼ **Some people could still afford large luxury cars.** This one even had a monogram on the door.

▲ A two-seater car could suddenly become a four-seater by opening the back and revealing the "rumble" or "dicky" seat.

◀ **Cars being serviced** in a 1920s garage workshop. It was no longer necessary for every motorist to be his own mechanic.

▲ **Early armoured vehicles** were often just ordinary cars which had been adapted for wartime use. The one in this photograph is a Ford Model T which has been fitted with a machine gun, though no protection has been provided for the soldiers using it.

▼ **Filling up** at an early kerbside petrol pump. These pumps delivered one, two or five gallons at a time. They were fed by large underground tanks which held as much as 1,000 gallons.

▼ **One of a few cars made in 1920 by a small coach-building firm in Coventry, England.** The firm bought ordinary mass-produced Morris Cowley chassis and constructed boat-shaped bodywork on them. They were two-seaters, so the four ladies were probably just posing in it for the picture.

# Gangsters and their Cars

On January 16, 1920 making, transporting and selling alcohol in any form was banned by law in America. The period that followed is often referred to as Prohibition. The law was supposed to have the effect of creating a new and greater America full of honest, sober and hard-working citizens. Instead it provided the criminal world with opportunities it had never had before. During the next ten years, the Federal authorities arrested half a million people for breaking this law.

## Al Capone

Large criminal gangs set up illegal breweries, bribed local police and "protected" the owners of clubs they sold liquor to. For the leaders of these gangs it was the most profitable crime they had ever been involved in. But it was dangerous too. Gangsters did not hesitate about killing a rival. So they had to protect themselves.

Two essential parts of a gangster's equipment were a car and a sub-machine gun, often called a "Chicago piano". Cars were used for getting away quickly and for protection against an enemy's bullets. Al Capone, a notorious American gangster of the 1920s, had an armour-plated car built specially for him.

▼ **Al Capone's armour-plated car was a V8 Cadillac built in 1928.** Cadillac had become one of America's top makers of luxury cars. The V8, which was first made in 1915, set new standards. It was smooth, silent, very comfortable and fast. It had the electric self-starter that Cadillac had introduced for the first time in 1912, and it had electric lights.

Capone's car had specially reinforced bodywork and windows to make it bulletproof. It weighed six tons – several times the weight of the standard model.

Engine had two banks of four cylinders arranged in a "V" shape – hence the name V8.

◄ **Bonnie Parker** who teamed up with Clyde Barrow to rob banks in America in the 1930s. The way they operated was to have one of their gang waiting outside the bank in a car with the engine running. They could then get quickly away with the money. The cars they used were usually stolen.

Hot air from engine escaped here.

► **Another special feature of Al Capone's car** was a hinged back window, which was used for firing guns at pursuing cars.

▼ **Police photograph of Al Capone.** He was born in Italy in 1895, but lived in America from the time he was one year old.

It is thought that Capone amassed a fortune of about 20 million dollars as a result of his crimes. When he was eventually arrested in 1931, the charge was income tax evasion. It has been estimated that he was responsible for the deaths of over 400 people but he always had alibis and nothing could be proved against him.

Thermostatically controlled radiator fins. As engine heated up they opened to allow more air in.

# Badges and Mascots

Over the years, most car manufacturers developed some kind of distinctive badge or insignia for their cars. Some had pictures to illustrate the firm's origins, others had purely fanciful designs.

A few car companies also developed their own distinctive radiator mascots, particularly those who made very luxurious cars. The Rolls-Royce company designed one for their cars because they disapproved of the personal mascots, such as gollywogs, which owners were buying and fitting on their cars themselves.

With the exception of Rolls-Royce, most of the badges on these pages can be seen only on cars in museums. The firms have either ceased to exist or merged with others.

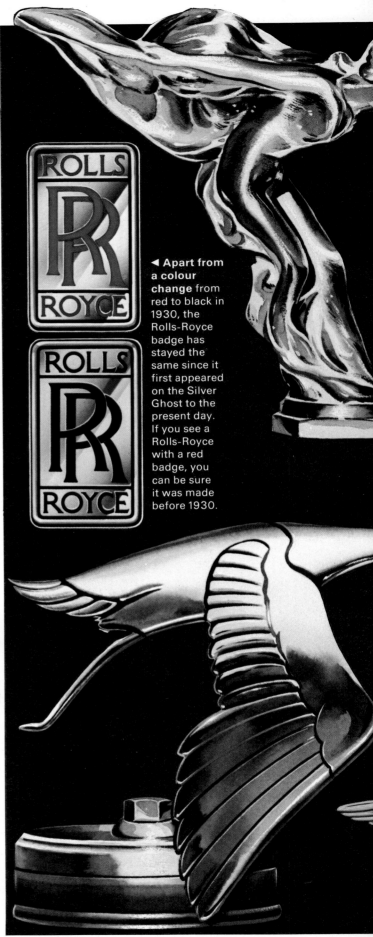

◄ **Apart from a colour change** from red to black in 1930, the Rolls-Royce badge has stayed the same since it first appeared on the Silver Ghost to the present day. If you see a Rolls-Royce with a red badge, you can be sure it was made before 1930.

▲ **This badge was used on Fiat cars** during the 1920s. The name was originally written F.I.A.T. because these letters were the initials of the company's name – Fabbrica Italiana Automobili Torino.

▲ **Like Fiat, the name Alfa came from the company's initials** – in this case Anonima Lombarda Fabbrica Automobili. Nicola Romeo, manager of the firm, also gave his name to the cars. The badge's cross and serpent come from the city arms of Milan.

▲ **Jowett of Britain** were one of several firms to use bird's wings on their badge. The Jowett brothers first made engines for other people's cars. They started making cars of their own in 1910. Their cars were quite popular, but their production methods and designs were outdated. They went out of business in the 1930s.

◄ **The Rolls-Royce mascot** was designed in 1911 by a British sculptor and commercial artist named Charles Sykes. From that time on, every Rolls-Royce customer had to buy one with his car. People who already owned a Rolls-Royce could obtain figures separately at the cost of a few pounds.

The lady varied somewhat from model to model and year to year. In 1938, she was kneeling. The particular mascot shown here was fitted to the Silver Ghost belonging to Lord Montague of Beaulieu.

Hispano-Suiza, the "Spanish-wiss" car company, took a tork as the symbol for their cars. he bird signified speed and egance of movement, and the uxury Hispano-Suizas of the 920s and 30s certainly lived up o its image. The wings of the bird vere repeated in the Hispano-uiza badge shown below.

The badge combines the two ountries' national colours – ed and yellow for Spain, red and hite for Switzerland.

▲ **The significance of this emblem** devised for the Stanley steam cars is uncertain, but the four horses probably show strength and speed. The emblem did not appear on all Stanley cars.

▲ **This Oldsmobile emblem** was used just before General Motors took over in 1920.

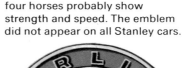

▲ **The earliest Belgian car manufacturers** took the name of the Roman goddess of wisdom, Minerva, for their cars and used her head on their emblem.

▲ **The American Locomotive Company** built the French Berliet cars under licence for a while, hence the picture on the badge. Berliet became part of Citroën.

▲ **The Panhard-Levassor emblem** shows the makers' initials. Some also had a letter "S" on each side, standing for *sans soupapes* – without valves.

◄ **The first Stutz cars** were made under the direction of Harry C. Stutz himself. When Harry left the company in 1919, his name stayed though a completely new line of cars was made by the new management. This emblem appeared on the first of these new Stutz cars. Again the symbol is wings, but this time very stylized.

◄ **Duesenberg produced the biggest,** fastest and most expensive American cars of the 1930s. This was the emblem for the luxurious Straight 8, so called because it had eight cylinders arranged in a single row.

# Part of Everyday Life

By the 1920s, cars had become much more reliable. People were able to set out on a long motor journey with a sense of confidence rather than adventure.

Horse-drawn vehicles had almost disappeared from towns. Road surfaces were much improved and traffic more organized than ever before. Most countries opted for one side of the road or the other and made vehicles keep to it by law. Traffic lights, road signs and policemen directed the flow of traffic, and pedestrians had learned to keep off the roads unless they wanted to cross over.

① Petrol pumps came into general use during the 1920s. Most had an electrically lit globe on the top. The pumps were hand-operated.

② More cars inevitably meant more accidents. Some garage owners equipped themselves with trucks fitted with cranes for towing broken-down cars.

③ Double-decker buses had motor engines by this time, but many were still open at the top.

④ Single-decker buses were used for long-distance travel between cities. Luggage was stacked outside next to the engine.

⑤ A mass-produced Citroën of 1922. Because of its colour this model was nicknamed *Citron Presse*, which means "lemonade".

⑥ Hydraulically operated dump truck. This was one of a wide variety of commercial and goods vehicles available by the 1920s.

⑦ Motorcycles, often with sidecars attached to carry passengers, were a very popular means of transport at this time. They were even cheaper than the small mass-produced cars.

⑧ This was one of the first models made by Bentley. It was made in Britain in 1920.

⑨ Herbert Austin began making small, cheap cars in 1922. They were known as Austin Sevens.

⑩ Despite the number of cheap mass-produced cars available during the 1920s, there were also a number of very large and luxurious cars around. This Kissel — an American car — was made in 1927.

The vehicles in this picture are not necessarily to scale.

German Presto of 1927

French taxi-cab

Model T
Ford

Large
delivery
van

6

10

7

3

1

9

American Buick
of 1925

45

# Time Chart

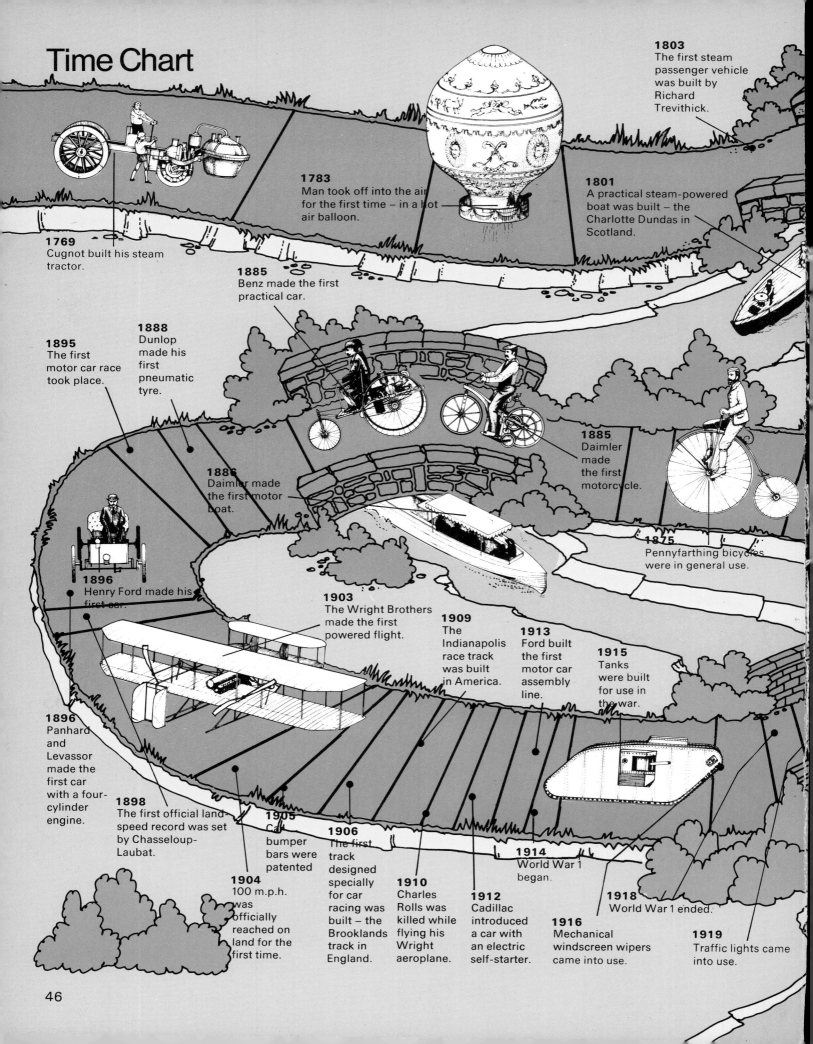

**1769**
Cugnot built his steam tractor.

**1783**
Man took off into the air for the first time — in a hot air balloon.

**1803**
The first steam passenger vehicle was built by Richard Trevithick.

**1801**
A practical steam-powered boat was built — the Charlotte Dundas in Scotland.

**1885**
Benz made the first practical car.

**1895**
The first motor car race took place.

**1888**
Dunlop made his first pneumatic tyre.

**1885**
Daimler made the first motor boat.

**1885**
Daimler made the first motorcycle.

**1875**
Pennyfarthing bicycles were in general use.

**1896**
Henry Ford made his first car.

**1903**
The Wright Brothers made the first powered flight.

**1909**
The Indianapolis race track was built in America.

**1913**
Ford built the first motor car assembly line.

**1915**
Tanks were built for use in the war.

**1896**
Panhard and Levassor made the first car with a four-cylinder engine.

**1898**
The first official land-speed record was set by Chasseloup-Laubat.

**1905**
Car bumper bars were patented

**1906**
The first track designed specially for car racing was built — the Brooklands track in England.

**1904**
100 m.p.h. was officially reached on land for the first time.

**1910**
Charles Rolls was killed while flying his Wright aeroplane.

**1912**
Cadillac introduced a car with an electric self-starter.

**1914**
World War 1 began.

**1916**
Mechanical windscreen wipers came into use.

**1918**
World War 1 ended.

**1919**
Traffic lights came into use.

46

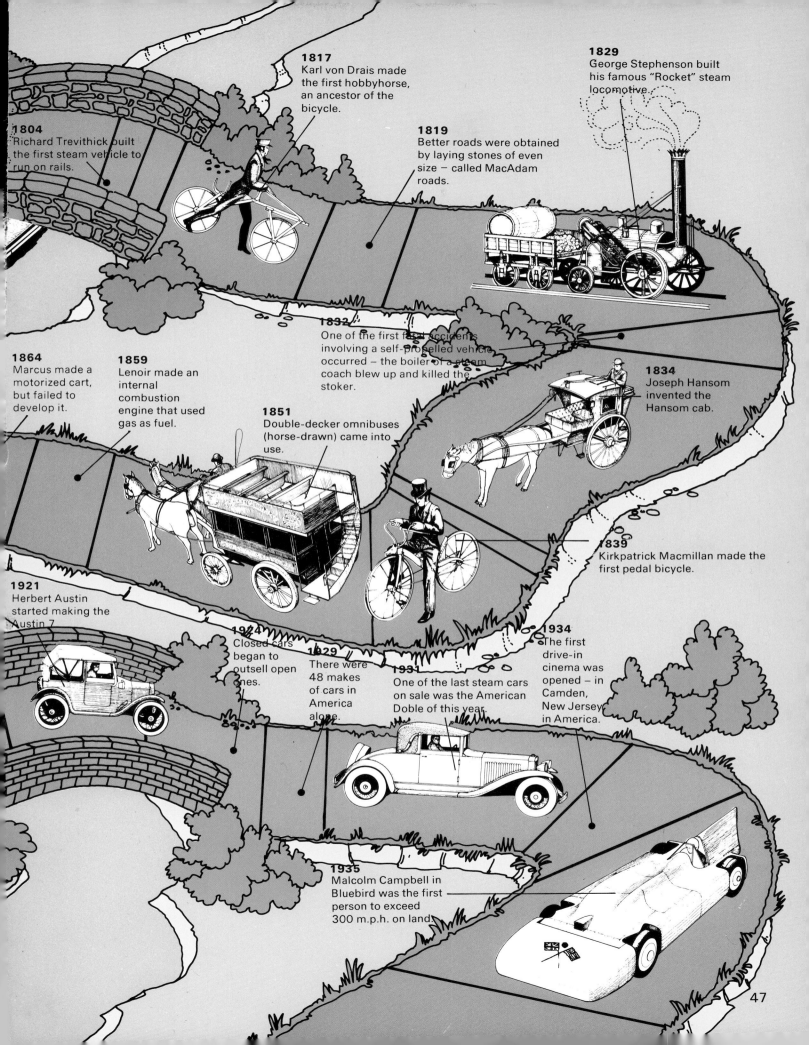

**1817**
Karl von Drais made the first hobbyhorse, an ancestor of the bicycle.

**1829**
George Stephenson built his famous "Rocket" steam locomotive.

**1804**
Richard Trevithick built the first steam vehicle to run on rails.

**1819**
Better roads were obtained by laying stones of even size – called MacAdam roads.

**1832**
One of the first fatal accidents involving a self-propelled vehicle occurred – the boiler of a steam coach blew up and killed the stoker.

**1864**
Marcus made a motorized cart, but failed to develop it.

**1859**
Lenoir made an internal combustion engine that used gas as fuel.

**1834**
Joseph Hansom invented the Hansom cab.

**1851**
Double-decker omnibuses (horse-drawn) came into use.

**1839**
Kirkpatrick Macmillan made the first pedal bicycle.

**1921**
Herbert Austin started making the Austin 7

**1924**
Closed cars began to outsell open ones.

**1929**
There were 48 makes of cars in America alone.

**1931**
One of the last steam cars on sale was the American Doble of this year.

**1934**
The first drive-in cinema was opened – in Camden, New Jersey, in America.

**1935**
Malcolm Campbell in Bluebird was the first person to exceed 300 m.p.h. on land.

# Index